SKEPTICAL

ESSAYS

S K E P T I C A L

E S S A Y S

B E N S O N   M A T E S

The University of Chicago Press • Chicago and London

The University of Chicago Press, Chicago 60637
The University of Chicago Press, Ltd., London

BENSON MATES is professor of philosophy
at the University of California, Berkeley.

Library of Congress Cataloging in Publication Data

Mates, Benson, 1919–
Skeptical essays.

Includes bibliographical references and index.
1. Skepticism—Addresses, essays, lectures.
2. Liar paradox—Addresses, essays, lectures.
3. Antinomy—Addresses, essays, lectures. 4. Free
will and determinism—Addresses, essays, lectures.
5. Knowledge, Theory of—Addresses, essays,
lectures. I. Title.
BD201.M34   149'.73   80–19553
ISBN 0–226–50986–9

To Lois

To Lois

C O N T E N T S

PREFACE

Traditional skepticism, as classically set forth in the writings of Sextus Empiricus, was primarily an epistemological doctrine. It held that we can only know how things *seem* to be; knowledge of how things really *are* is impossible. "For example, honey appears to us to be sweet—this we grant, for we perceive sweetness [literally, we are sweetened] through the senses. But whether it *is* sweet, as it is said to be, we doubt." Hence the skeptic considers that the right attitude toward questions concerning the true nature of things is suspension of judgment, which in turn is supposed to give rise to a highly desirable state of blessed imperturbability, or *ataraxia*.

The skepticism expressed in the following essays goes beyond the traditional form in certain respects. It is directed in the first instance to all the major problems of philosophy, only one of which—the so-called External World problem—constituted almost the entire subject matter of the traditional doctrine. It doubts that these problems are solvable or even "dissolvable"; and, somewhat adapting the ancient slogan *Ou mallon* ("no more this than that"), it argues that the reasons given on both sides of the issues are equally good and not, as suggested in antiquity, equally bad. In response to the relatively recent view that, although the problems are indeed insoluble, this is only because they do not make sense, it finds that they make at least as good sense as most of what passes for sense in the discourse of everyday life.

As for *ataraxia*, I find no evidence that skepticism leads to any such desirable state. On the contrary, the rational minds among us are not inclined to give up the struggle, while the rest become religious mystics or philosophical obscurantists, neither condition seriously describable as "blessed."

Sextus, in a simile later borrowed without acknowledgment by Wittgenstein, suggests that, just as a man who has climbed to a high place may afterwards kick over the ladder by which he ascended, so also the skeptic can afterwards demolish the very arguments by which he has supported his skepticism. To reinforce this idea, he gives us additional similes, too, perhaps the most graphic of them being the cathartic that, after flushing out everything else, flushes itself out as well. This self-destructive power of skepticism was perhaps what was supposed to result eventually in *ataraxia*. But it doesn't seem to work.

We have also to recognize that skepticism, though it is indispensable to philosophy, is not an outlook or habit of mind that is much approved by the majority of mankind. People want solutions—"positive contributions"—not arguments to show that no solutions are likely ever to be found. Even the "optimistic" skeptical doctrine advanced here, according to which all the participants in the principal philosophical disputes are right (except insofar as they assert that their opponents are wrong), has not proved to be much more congenial than ordinary Pyrrhonism; in philosophy we have learned to get our satisfaction from showing that the other fellow is mistaken rather than from establishing the truth of our own positive tenets.

Although the doubts expressed in these essays are meant to be very general, extending to all the purported solutions and dissolutions that have been proposed for all the major philosophical problems, it must be obvious that it would be far beyond anyone's ability (to say nothing of the reader's patience) to survey the entire field *in extenso*. Instead, I have chosen two main problems as examples. Even in regard to these I probably have failed to discuss the reader's favorite ways of dealing with them. But perhaps what I have written will at least reinforce his opinion that the more or less standard approaches do not succeed.

This work has been in soak for a long time, longer than its quality might suggest. The central idea was sketched in a paper, "Philosophical Scepticism and the Logical Antinomies," published in the *Proceedings of the XIV International Congress of Philosophy*, and some of the material on the External World problem was published in my paper, "Sense Data" (*Inquiry*, vol. 10, 1967). I owe a debt of gratitude to the many students and colleagues who have tried, kindly but unsuccessfully, to cure me of my doubts; I feel a strong urge to apologize to them for being so obtuse, even though I think that I am right about the issues. Finally, I should like to express my appreciation to the John Simon Guggenheim Memorial Foundation for the fellowship that allowed me to complete the book this year.

SKEPTICAL
ESSAYS

INTRODUCTION

The principal traditional problems of philosophy are
genuine intellectual knots; they are intelligible enough,
but at the same time they are absolutely insoluble. This is
the thesis I propose to support in the skeptical essays that
follow.

Paradigms of what I call "genuine intellectual knots" are
the antinomies of logic and semantics. The first essay
examines a pair of these, namely, the Liar and Russell's
Antinomy, with the aim of nailing down the fact that such
knots do exist and are not merely the product of careless
and confused reasoning. After that sobering reminder,
subsequent essays consider two of the most notorious
traditional problems of philosophy, those of Free Will and
Our Knowledge of the External World, showing that they
are like the aforementioned antinomies in certain essential
respects.

The term *antinomy*, as used here, denotes any argument
that has a self-contradictory conclusion and yet seems to
be logically valid and to have only necessary truths as
premises. Accordingly, the antinomies constitute a subclass of the *paradoxes*, which may be defined as seemingly
valid arguments that obtain implausible conclusions from

plausible premises (or that obtain, from given premises, conclusions seemingly independent of those premises). This distinction needs further sharpening, but for our present purpose, which is only to take notice of certain general similarities between philosophical problems and two particular antinomies, the foregoing characterization will suffice. It should be noticed, however, that any antinomy can equivalently be presented in the form of a pair of seemingly valid arguments, one leading to one side of the contradiction, the other to the other, and each having only necessary truths as premises. This is closer to the situation in philosophy, where usually one side of the contradiction is considered so obvious as hardly to need any supporting argumentation, and all attention is focused on the argument leading to the other.

The marks of a good, mind-graveling antinomy are that the argument should be reasonably short, that its logical transitions should satisfy standards as high as are imposed on reasoning anywhere else, and that its premises should seem clearly true by virtue of the very meaning of their constituent terms. To the extent that any of these criteria are not met, the argument will fail to occasion much intellectual discomfort. For, after all, it is no surprise that with sloppy enough reasoning and woolly enough terminology one can obtain conclusions of any sort whatever, even contradictions, the probability of such an unfortunate result increasing with the length of the argument. In order for us to feel properly cornered by an antinomy there must apparently be no way out; so long as we can suspect that there is a gap in the reasoning or that one of the premises just might not be true, we can regard the deduction of a contradiction as merely an indication that one or both of these deficiencies is present.

Similar considerations hold in the case of philosophical problems. A "good" problem—i.e., a problem that is worth the kind of intense intellectual effort that philosophers devote to their subject—consists primarily of a short, simple, seemingly sound argument that leads from apparently incontrovertible premises to an extremely paradoxical conclusion. It typically gives rise to all sorts of purported solutions: each and every step in the argument is challenged by someone as concealing a logical fallacy; every term that occurs is found by someone to be vague or ambiguous; every premise is deemed by one scholar or another to be controvertible after all. And sometimes, after the philosopher has run through the seemingly sound argument enough times, he may finally decide, under its pressure, that the conclusion is not really so paradoxical as at first it appeared to be. Or, in another very common but even less satisfactory way of responding, he simply rehearses the argument or arguments in favor of the opposite conclusion, as though that would suffice to lay the puzzle to rest.

What makes both the antinomies and the philosophical problems so interesting, and what keeps them going, is the fact that, although each possible point of contact is identified by somebody as the source of the difficulty, each is also exonerated by the great majority; and consequently no purported solution ever comes close to general acceptance.

It will be obvious that the thesis of these essays places certain requirements on their style and manner. If they are to have any chance of persuading the gentle but properly skeptical reader that the philosophical problems they discuss are both intelligible and insoluble, it will be necessary that at every stage all the cards be laid face up on the table. Or to vary the metaphor, the reader must not be diverted by any semantic sleight-of-hand or other deceptive tricks while the rabbit of paradox is being brought out of the hat; on the contrary, he must be encouraged to give the closest possible attention to the hat, the rabbit, and every other essential feature of the performance.

There must be no surprises (other than the big surprise that such strange conclusions could follow from such innocuous premises); fancy terminology must be held to a minimum; and, above all, the argumentation must never become so hazy that, when the paradoxical conclusion finally appears, we can escape its force simply by telling ourselves that somewhere in the philosophical fog an unnoticed logical leap must have been made.

As examples of antinomies to be examined and appreciated, I have chosen the Liar and Russell's Antinomy because they both have the aforementioned qualities of brevity, clarity, simplicity, and logical toughness. The Liar, not to be confused with the paradox about the Cretan prophet Epimenides, was stated in antiquity in the following form:

> When a man says "What I am now saying is false," what he says is both true and false.

A sharper formulation, by W. V. Quine, utilizes the predicate "yields a falsehood when appended to its own quotation," a predicate that, e.g., is true of the words "is a noun" and false of the words "is a phrase." The result of appending this predicate to its own quotation, namely,

> "Yields a falsehood when appended to its own quotation" yields a falsehood when appended to its own quotation.[1]

is a sentence easily shown to be true if and only if it is not true. Thus, the antinomy of the Liar, in this version, will be a seemingly valid argument that, although its premises are necessary truths, has as its conclusion the contradiction that the sentence displayed above is true if and only if it is not true.

Russell's Antinomy, in its most usual formulation, concerns the class of all classes that are not members of themselves. This class is a member of itself if and only if it is not a member of itself. Another version may be constructed about the property P of being a nonself-applicable property. The property P belongs, e.g., to the property "belongs to everything," for "belongs to everything" does not belong to everything (since it does not even belong to all properties). On the other hand, P does not belong to the property "is identical with itself," because that property *is* identical with itself and hence is self-applicable. But does the property P belong to itself? The answer, of course, is that P belongs to P if and only if P does not belong to P.

When it comes to the possibility of solutions for these and the other logical and semantic antinomies, there is a parting of the ways between the optimists and the pessimists. The optimists think that all of them will be solved in due course (if indeed they have not been solved already) and that, although hundreds or even thousands of years may pass before the solutions are widely accepted as "intuitive," since they probably will involve a repudiation of part of what may be called "our conceptual heritage," they will in the end seem as right and as obvious as the usual solutions to Zeno's paradoxes seem today. "One man's antinomy," says Quine, "is another man's paradox, give or take a couple of thousand years."[2]

The pessimists, including the present author, consider it more likely that no intuitive solutions to such antinomies as Russell's and the Liar will *ever* be found. The Liar, in particular, has been under scrutiny for at least twenty-four hundred years, and, although all this attention has led to a number of interesting distinctions and other results, we should scarcely exaggerate if we said that there does not appear to have been one iota of progress toward a generally acceptable solution. Incidentally, the case is quite unlike that of Zeno's paradoxes, which probably never were thought to be antinomies anyway. In regard to them, even Aristotle observes that, just as the space between here and the goal is said by Zeno to consist of an infinite succession of intervals each of which is half as long as its predecessor, so the associated interval of time will consist of an infinite succession of intervals each of which is of half the duration of its predecessor; Aristotle then holds that Zeno is consequently in the position of arguing that, although an infinite succession of space intervals can add up to a finite space, an infinite succession of intervals of time must add up to an infinite time.[3] Granted that this is not the full solution (*that* is given by the theory of convergent series), most people would nevertheless agree that Aristotle has at least found the locus of the fallacy. But with the Liar the situation is quite different. Despite centuries of effort by the best minds, no cure has yet been proposed that is not worse than the disease.

Russell's Antinomy, though much younger than the Liar, shows all the signs of being similarly resistant to solution. Every juncture in every form of the argument has been minutely examined and has been identified by one writer or another as the source of the difficulty. We again have the characteristic situation in which everyone agrees that *something* is wrong but there is no consensus as to *what* is wrong. Some say that the expression "x is a member of x" is not meaningful at all and that its negation is consequently not meaningful either; others find that the latter is meaningful enough but deny that there exists a class of those and only those things that satisfy it; still others grant the existence of such a class but say that it cannot be a member of anything; and so on. Each way out seems unintuitive to most people; each way exacts its own exorbitant price by introducing *ad hoc* restrictions that create complications where simplicity ought to reign.

It is not my purpose to attempt to *demonstrate* in some way that these antinomies not only have not been solved but are actually insoluble. By what procedure such a thesis could be established in these cases, where some of the most fundamental concepts of logic itself are at stake, is far from clear. I wish only to draw the clearheaded reader's attention to the fact that there can be cases in which the argumentation on both sides of an issue is logically impeccable (i.e., at least as good as argumentation upon which we depend in cases that no one would challenge) and where neither the argument pro nor the argument con rests on any premise that can plausibly be given up in order to avoid the conclusion. As we see with special clarity in the antinomies, such cases can be expected to exhibit two important features:

(a) There will be nearly unanimous agreement that *something* is wrong; but nevertheless, though every student of the subject will have his or her own favorite solution, none of the purported solutions will command the assent of more than a small proportion of those concerned.

(b) It is futile to attempt to discredit the argument for one side of the issue by rehearsing the good argument for the other side; indeed, that's the whole trouble: there are good arguments on *both* sides.

I think it obvious that most of the major traditional problems show these same marks; in fact, the more carefully they are formulated, the more they look like antinomies or tough paradoxes. Each of these problems may of course be formulated in many different ways, as will be emphasized when we come to the detailed discussion of those concerning Free Will and the External World. With respect to one typical way of setting up the Free Will problem, for example, the corresponding particular instance of my thesis would go roughly as follows: any plausible definitions of the terms "freedom" and "moral responsibility" will yield the unacceptable conclusion that, if one is morally responsible for only such acts as one does freely, then no one is morally responsible for anything whatever. Similarly in the case of the External World problem, the more carefully we define our terms and the more sharply we formulate the problem, the more inexorably we are led to the conclusion that we have no justification at all for belief in the existence of anything other than our own immediate experience. I am not saying

9

that these or any other philosophical problems have yet been stated with the preciseness found in some formulations of the logical antinomies, but only that, as they are continually examined and restated (in response to purported solutions and dissolutions), the successive formulations seem gradually to converge toward arguments of an antinomy-like character.

Of course there are certain obvious and perhaps deeply significant differences. A logical antinomy is usually presented either as an argument with a contradiction as a conclusion or as a pair of arguments such that the conclusion of one contradicts that of the other. But the typical philosophical problem, as we have earlier noted, takes the form of an argument to establish a conclusion that contradicts something "obviously" true. Thus, when one is given arguments to show that nobody is morally responsible for any of his acts or that we have no basis for belief in the existence of an external world, no arguments are offered for the opposite conclusions, as these are considered almost self-evident. Further, in the philosophical cases there are often premises of questionable status as regards necessity or contingency, as, for example, the premise that every event is the effect of antecedent causes or the assumption that it is at least logically possible for our experience to be as it is even if no external world exists. So one must grant that the philosophical problems do differ from the logical antinomies in at least these respects, as well as in the relatively low degree of precision with which they are frequently formulated. Nevertheless, I maintain that the similarity is close enough to justify our expecting that the philosophical problems, like the antinomies, will continue to exhibit features (a) and (b) above.

The applicability of (a) to the solutions and dissolutions offered up to now is so obvious that it will hardly be disputed. The applicability of (b) is sometimes overlooked in practice. For instance, the traditional arguments claiming to show the impossibility of knowledge of other minds are in no way sufficiently answered by making such declarations (with liberal use of italics and other types of emphasis) as "*Of course* I *do* sometimes know that Tom is angry." We must reply, "Yes, *of course* you *do;* but now please explain exactly what is wrong with the proof that this is not so." Again, let no one tell us that "*Of course* we *are* morally responsible for much of what we do, else we would not even know what terms 'responsibility' and 'freedom' mean—so that there *must* be something wrong with the argument to the contrary"; for we want to know just *what* is wrong with that argument.

The real trouble is that no specific attempt to solve any one of these problems, i.e., to pick out the fallacy, has ever succeeded. Either the proposed solution has been found to rest on premises that themselves lack adequate intuitive or other support, or the problem has been rephrased until the particular aspect under attack—whether it be the validity of the argument or the truth or meaningfulness of its constituent sentences—has been brought to a condition at least as satisfactory as one finds in other argumentation that no one would dream of challenging.

The two philosophical problems I have chosen for detailed examination, although they are prime examples of the kind of enigmas that have occupied philosophers for centuries, exhibit a certain interesting difference. The Free Will problem, unlike the other, has an obvious importance outside of philosophy. Its essential observation, that, the more clearly and extensively we can trace out the causal sequences leading to a given action, the less we are inclined to assign praise or blame for that action, is illustrated constantly in the deliberations of judges, juries, and other groups entrusted with the task of apportioning rewards and punishments.

This was clearly exemplified in two recent and highly publicized cases in California. In one instance a young heiress was kidnapped by a band of barbarous fanatics and subjected to severe physical and mental mistreatment;

she later took part with them in robbing a bank, and she was eventually brought to trial and convicted of this "crime." There was great public uneasiness about the verdict. Many people saw a basic injustice in punishing someone for doing what almost *anyone*, subjected to such terrible treatment, would probably have done, while on the other side there was a dim awareness, I suppose, that, if you once begin to take the causes of a person's choices into account, there will be no place to draw the line rationally and every criminal act will have its exculpatory circumstances.

In the other case a San Francisco supervisor shot and killed the mayor and another supervisor. Here the defense managed to focus the jury's attention on the antecedent circumstances that presumably caused the accused to do what he did. His disappointments, his anger, his confusion, his depression, even his poor antecedent diet, were brought into consideration. The result was that he was given a far milder penalty than would have been expected. Again there was strong public dissatisfaction with the outcome, this time caused, in part at least, by the feeling that on these terms *anyone*, no matter how heinous the crime, could be partially or completely exonerated. In both cases the Free Will problem is plainly to be seen in the background: on the one hand, it cannot be denied that we must take into account the causes of people's choices and of their subsequent actions; on the other, there would seem to be no limit to the exculpatory force of this unless we are willing to make the *agent's* responsibility or lack of it depend somehow upon *our* relative ignorance or knowledge of why he has done what he has done.

The External World problem, on the other hand, seems to have no such practical implications. Indeed, one of its most puzzling aspects is precisely that, if what it puts forward as logically possible were actually the case—i.e., if there existed nothing beyond our perceptions and yet these same perceptions occurred in the same order as they do now—no one would notice the difference. The so-called External World "never would be missed," as it were; we would have exactly as much basis as we do now for asserting the existence of a world of things independent of our perceptions, and yet that assertion would be false. It is a platitude among philosophers that Dr. Johnson and other people who thought they could refute Berkeley by demonstratively kicking stones or by inviting him to exit the room through the wall merely showed thereby their failure to grasp the content of what he was saying. Properly understood, the hypothesis that nothing exists besides our perceptions seems to have no verifiable consequences whatsoever, and therefore we can hardly expect any practical problems to issue from the possibility of its truth.

At any rate, despite such differences in practical effect, the Free Will and External World problems seem typical of the conundrums that have puzzled philosophers down through the centuries. But, even for these two, to survey and assess all the ingenious attempts that have been made to solve or dissolve them would be an enormous undertaking, far beyond my capability and intent. The more modest goal of the following essays is only to set forth some of the considerations that have persuaded me that the reason why philosophical problems are not solved is that, like the antinomies we shall consider, they are insoluble though intelligible. They are conceptual knots that cannot be undone.

TWO ANTINOMIES

The Liar

According to ancient tradition, the antinomy of the Liar
was discovered by Eubulides of Miletus, a follower of the
philosopher Euclid, who in turn was a contemporary of
Socrates and founded the Megarian school of logicians.[1] If
this tradition is correct, the event took place sometime
around the middle of the fourth century B.C. We do not
know in exactly what form the antinomy was stated by
Eubulides, but evidently by the end of that century it was
much discussed and was taken very seriously. Athenaeus
reports that the poet and grammarian Philetas (*ca.* 340–285
B.C.), a resident of the beautiful Aegean island of Cos,
worried so much about the antinomy that for lack of sleep
he became increasingly emaciated and finally perished, as
attested by the epitaph on his gravestone:

> O Stranger: Philetas of Cos am I,
> 'Twas the Liar who made me die,
> And the bad nights caused thereby.[2]

Athenaeus elsewhere supplements this report with the
information that before his death Philetas became so thin

that he had to attach lead weights to his feet to keep from being blown over by the strong Coan winds. So perhaps we are dealing with more than one Liar here; but anyway it makes a good story, and it certainly shows that the antinomy was notorious at a very early date.

There is some evidence that Theophrastus (*ca.* 371–287 B.C.), Aristotle's successor as head of the Peripatetic school, wrote three books (papyrus rolls) on the Liar,[3] and the Stoic philosopher Chrysippus (*ca.* 280–205 B.C.) is reported by Diogenes Laertius to have devoted at least six works to the subject.[4] Diogenes lists these under such tantalizing titles as "On the Liar, to Aristocreon, six books" (Aristocreon was Chrysippus's nephew and favorite student); "Against those who think that some propositions are both true and false, one book"; "Against those who solve the Liar by division, to Aristocreon, two books"; "Against those who maintain that the premises of the Liar are false, one book"; not to mention "Introduction to the Liar, to Aristocreon, one book," and "Liar arguments, an introduction, one book." Unfortunately, we have no other hints as to the contents of these works.

Actual formulations of the Liar do not occur in the extant literature prior to Cicero (106–43 B.C.). He gives several, none of which is quite right.[5] In one place, after gaining the reader's assent to "If you say that it is now light and tell the truth, then it is now light," he proposes "If you say that you are lying and tell the truth, then you are lying." This, as will be seen, is only half of the antinomy. Elsewhere he does somewhat better, with the question "If you say you are lying and you tell the truth, are you lying or telling the truth?" The first formulation that can be considered really correct is ascribed to the Aristotelian commentator Alexander of Aphrodisias (*fl. ca.* A.D. 200), but it may very well be much later: "The man who says 'I am lying' is both lying and telling the truth."[6]

From these early times down to the present there has been almost uninterrupted discussion of the Liar by philosophers. And in general it can be said that, the stronger a given period was philosophically, the more intense and voluminous the discussion has been. In the Middle Ages the Liar was called "The Insoluble." Paul of Venice listed fifteen different solutions he had heard of, and the problem was treated by Ockham, Buridan, and all the other major figures.[7] In modern times the literature has become so extensive as practically to require a professional bibliographer for its survey.[8]

Recent authors often confuse the Liar with a paradox they have dubbed "the Epimenides," derived from a passage in the New Testament. Saint Paul, warning his representative, Titus, about the difficulties that would have to be faced in bringing the inhabitants of Crete to the true faith, wrote, "It was a Cretan prophet, one of their own countrymen, who said 'Cretans are always liars, vicious brutes, lazy gluttons'—and he told the truth!"[9] It is conjectured that the reference was to Epimenides, a semilegendary prophet and poet who was a sort of Cretan Rip Van Winkle, sleeping away 57 years of his life in a cave and living to the ripe old age of 157 (or, according to the Cretans, 299).[10] Saint Paul gives no indication of regarding his statement to Titus as paradoxical, but recent authors, taking it in the sense of "Epimenides, the Cretan, said 'Everything said by Cretans is false,'" have noticed the puzzle. For, if what Epimenides said is true, it is false; therefore, it *is* false; therefore, at least one other statement by a Cretan is true. We do not have an antinomy here, for no contradiction has been derived; but we do have a proof of the curious and implausible result that, if Epimenides happened to make the false statement attributed to him, then some Cretan must have said something true.[11]

Returning to the Liar, let us now consider proposals for solving it. To give a systematic survey of all the attempts at solution that have been made in recent times is well-nigh impossible because of the large number of ways in which the antinomy and its near relatives have been formulated and because every step of every one of these formulations has been fixed upon by someone as the source of the difficulty. As points of reference for our discussion, however, we may consider initially the following versions.

1. If a man says "I am lying," what he says is true if and only if it is false.

2. The sentence

This sentence is false

is true if and only if it is false.

3. Let the letter "*A*" abbreviate the phrase "the sentence appearing on line 13 of page 18 of *Skeptical Essays*," and consider the sentence

A is not true.

Now, just as we have, by the very meaning of "true,"

"It is snowing" is true if and only if it is snowing,

so we also have

(*i*) "*A* is not true" is true if and only if *A* is not true.

But by inspection we see that the following is the case:

(*ii*) *A* = "*A* is not true."

Therefore, by substitution in (*i*) on the basis of (*ii*), we obtain

(*iii*) *A* is true if and only if *A* is not true.

Of these three formulations, only the first strictly deserves the ancient appellation, "The Liar." To get the contradiction, we must of course understand "I am lying" to refer to itself. But what sort of thing are we speaking of here; i.e., what is this "it"?

Many philosophers of language nowadays propose to distinguish three kinds of entities, namely, sentences, propositions, and statements.[12] A (declarative) *sentence* is a linguistic expression; it consists of a sequence of words, and in almost all cases it belongs to one language only. By contrast, a *proposition* is said to be a meaning or thought that is capable of being expressed by one or more sentences, possibly in different languages. And a *statement* is neither a sentence nor the meaning of a sentence but something that is "made" when a sentence is uttered in certain favorable circumstances. Thus, the sentences "It is raining" and "Es regnet" are obviously different but nevertheless express the same proposition and hence are intertranslatable; either sentence could be used to make an infinity of different statements at different times and places or, under appropriate conditions, could be used to make the same statement that would be made, for example, by uttering the sentence "It is raining in Berkeley, California, on December 19, 1979," with which neither of them is synonymous.

If we accept this distinction, we have to ask whether the Liar has to do with a sentence, a proposition, or a statement. Instantly a great proliferation of versions appears, involving, e.g., "This sentence is false," "This proposition is false," "This statement is false," "The proposition expressed by this sentence is false," "The statement I am now making by uttering this sentence is false," etc. Some of these formulations seem at first glance to point a way out of the antinomy; e.g., if I say "This statement is false," it may be replied that, although I have uttered a sentence, I have failed to make a statement thereby, and hence the words "This statement," in the present situation, have no referent. Unfortunately, as we shall see later, this type of approach, like all the others, leads into a thicket of conflicting intuitions from which there is no satisfactory exit.

We may as well begin, therefore, by considering some such formulation as 2, above, which takes sentences, instead of propositions or statements, as the bearers of truth and falsehood. This is, moreover, the form that is discussed in most of the recent treatments of the subject.

Two features of this particular formulation are patently accidental and probably should be altered in order to remove the temptation of trying to base a solution upon them. The first is the locution "this sentence," which may appear suspect because in the present context, unlike what we find in more ordinary cases, it cannot be eliminated by replacing it by the quotation-name of the sentence to which it refers. (If we try such an elimination here, we get only

"This sentence is false" is false,

which is no longer self-referential in the way required for producing the antinomy.)[13] Consequently, in order to dispose of purported solutions that attach some deep significance to this phenomenon, let us give the Liar sentence a different way of referring to itself. And, while we are at it, we may as well replace "false" by "not true." This will have the advantage of clarifying the problem somewhat for those who believe that some sentences are neither true nor false and who therefore may find no contradiction in the conclusion that the Liar sentence is true if and only if it is false.

That brings us to formulation 3, due essentially to Łukasiewicz via Tarski.[14] As is the case with all other formulations of which I am aware, each step of this one is challenged by some people but is accepted by most.

Analyzing the assumptions that lead to the antinomy as thus formulated, Tarski writes as follows:

(I) We have implicitly assumed that the language in which the antinomy is constructed contains, in addition to its expressions, also the names of these expressions, as well as semantic terms such as the term "true" referring to sentences of this language; we have also assumed that all sentences which determine the adequate usage of this term can be asserted in the language ... A language with these properties will be called "semantically closed."

(II) We have assumed that in this language the ordinary laws of logic hold.

(III) We have assumed that we can formulate and assert in our language an empirical premise such as the statement *(ii)* which has occurred in our argument.

Tarski notes that the last assumption is inessential, for the antinomy can be reformulated in such a way as to avoid the use of any empirical premise.[15]

This analysis suggests a framework for classifying the multifarious attempts that have been made to resolve the antinomy. First, there is a large family of proposals that are directed toward assumption (I) and endeavor in various ways to introduce plausible restrictions preventing the language from being semantically closed. Another approach, which seems to be gaining adherents in recent times, is to challenge assumption (II) by arguing, e.g., that the logic of the natural language is best regarded as multivalued, or as characterized by "truth-value gaps," or that Leibniz's Law fails for the context " . . . is true." Finally, there is a group of purported solutions utilizing what I shall call "the retreat into the abstract." These take the line that propositions, or statements, or judgments, and in any case not sentences, are properly the bearers of truth and falsehood. Accordingly, they allege that the Liar sentence, i.e., *A*, involves some sort of category mistake and is therefore nonsensical. They assure us further, on grounds never made clear, that the sentence

> The proposition expressed by this sentence is false

does not express a proposition and that if we utter the sentence

> The statement made by uttering this sentence here and now is false

we shall have failed to make a statement. Likewise, it is supposed to be impossible to express a judgment by saying

> The judgment I express by uttering this
> sentence is false,

for allegedly there is no such judgment.

The three types of approach just described are by no means mutually exclusive, and many attempted solutions appear to fall under two, or even all three, of these headings. Nevertheless, the indicated classification will serve at least to bring some order into our consideration of the possibilities.

BLOCKING SEMANTIC CLOSURE

Perhaps the most radical proposal of the first type comes from the direction of Wittgenstein's *Tractatus,* where it *seems* to be held (though nothing is clear) that no meaningful sentence can be about itself.[16] Sentences (or propositions—at this point in his work the distinction is not being noticed) are said to *show* but not to *describe* their own "logical" properties.[17] The idea seems to be that a sentence is a sort of pictorial sign for the state of affairs it describes and must contain component pictorial signs for the components of that state of affairs; if it were about itself, it would have to be a rather odd picture that contained a picture of itself. Since understanding a sentence is then supposed to be something like knowing what state of affairs it is a picture of, any attempt to understand one of these self-referential sentences would seem to lead to a regress: in our perusal of the picture P, in order to figure out what it is a picture of, we would find that it contained a subpicture P' that was an exact miniature duplicate of P; and P' in turn would contain a still smaller picture P'', which would need to be understood in order to understand P', and so on ad infinitum. Some simile such as this is probably behind the notion that it is impossible for a sentence—i.e., a meaningful, intelligible sentence—to be about itself.

But so much the worse for the simile, for there are many, many examples in the natural languages of sentences that are obviously about themselves. When the small boy in Germany asks you to say something in English, you respond with

Now I am speaking English,

what you have said is perfectly meaningful and true.

This is a sentence in English

is true, and so is

This is a true sentence in English,

while

This is a sentence in French

is false. Each of these sentences is self-referential, but each is as clear and unambiguous as any other sentence we meet in ordinary discourse. When reading an English grammar that is written in English, we account it a rather comical fault on the part of the author if he does not manage to follow the rules he states. And a manual of style that advised

Never use a preposition to end a sentence with

would, for at least two reasons, deserve to be thrown into the wastebasket.

To this must be added the fact that artificial languages have been constructed that are consistent and allow the formulation of their own syntax. Indeed, Gödel's famed incompleteness proof consisted in showing that we can associate numbers with the expressions of elementary arithmetic and logic in such a way that, for any given consistent set of arithmetical axioms, there will always be a sentence saying that its own number is not the number of a sentence derivable from those axioms, i.e., a sentence saying (truly) of itself that it is not a formal consequence of the axioms.

Thus, the wholesale exclusion of sentences that are about themselves is a measure drastically at odds with our basic intuitions about what can be said; we see no reason why we should not make a perfectly meaningful remark that applies, even uniquely, to itself.

In this connection, it is worth noting that whether a given sentence refers to itself, or refers to itself uniquely, is not in general decidable by mere inspection of its intrinsic syntactical features, for it may depend on the features of other sentences or on certain empirical matters of fact. The sentence "Every English sentence asserted by Mates contains fewer than 100 words" is self-referential only if I happen to assert it. The sentence "The first sentence that is mentioned on this page and begins with the word 'the' is false" is uniquely self-referential or not depending upon which other sentences I happen to mention (not use) on this page. Again, suppose that we start writing sentences on a series of numbered cards, one sentence on each card; on card 1 we write "The sentence on card 2 is true"; on card 2 we write "The sentence on card 3 is true"; and so on for a while. If on some card n we happen to write "The sentence on card 1 is not true," our first sentence, and indeed each of the others, suddenly becomes self-referential in the way that leads into the antinomy. Whether or not that first sentence is self-referential cannot be determined by looking at it alone but plainly depends upon what is written subsequently. For one last example, let the letter "P" abbreviate any empirical sentence, e.g., "January 1, 2000, will be a bright, sunny day in Berkeley," and then consider the following sentence:

> The sentence that is this sentence if P, and
> is "$1 = 1$" otherwise, is false.

Whether this asserts its own falsehood depends upon the weather in the year 2000, which presumably cannot be determined by any investigation, however profound, of English syntax and semantics.

Since wholesale exclusion of self-referential sentences is too drastic a remedy for the Liar, we must next consider criteria for the applicability of the particular predicates "true" and "false," with the hope of finding in that direction some plausible basis for excluding the bad actors.

Approaching the problem from this side, we have several proposals to ponder. The most drastic, again, is the so-called no-truth theory. According to it, asserting a sentence like

"It is snowing" is true

is just another way, possibly more emphatic, of asserting the corresponding sentence

It is snowing.

Generalized, the proposal is to regard each sentence of the form "Q is true," where Q is the quotation-name of a sentence S, as equivalent, by definition, to S. The proper role of the pseudo-predicate "is true," according to this, is not to express a genuine attribute of sentences or anything else but only to serve as a kind of exclamation point.[18] Since it plainly is not playing that kind of role in the Liar sentence, the Liar sentence is nonsense and the antinomy is eliminated.

Unfortunately for this idea, however, many obviously unproblematic occurrences of the predicate "is true" are not accompanied by quotation-names of sentences; consider, for example, the sentences

Most of Smith's testimony is true.
The first sentence in Herodotus's *History* is true.
All consequences of true sentences are true.

Hence, the proposal does not provide a way of eliminating "true" and "false" from our vocabulary, and in particular it offers us no help whatsoever with the Liar.

A less drastic proposal, which does offer some help, is that of assigning levels $0, 1, 2, \ldots, n, \ldots$, to our sentences and replacing the single predicate "true" by an infinite sequence of predicates "true_1," "true_2," $\ldots$, "true_n," $\ldots$, in such a way that the predicate "true_m" occurs only in sentences of level m or higher and is meaningfully applicable only to sentences of level $m - 1$ or lower.[19] Thus, level 0 might consist of sentences in which no truth-predicate (or other semantic predicate) occurs. The truth-predicate "true_1" would apply to these. Level 1 would consist of all sentences of level 0 together with such additional sentences as could be formed by adding the predicate "true_1" to the stock of predicates already occurring. For that level we would have a new truth-predicate, "true_2." Then we could construct level 2 by taking the sentences of level 1 together with the result of adding "true_2" to our stock of predicates. For level 2 there would be another truth-predicate, "true_3." And so on.

On this basis, an expression of the form "S is true_n" will be meaningful only if the sentence or sentences referred to are of level no higher than $n - 1$. In particular, for no n will it be possible meaningfully to affirm or deny "true_n" of a sentence containing that predicate. Thus the Liar sentence goes out, and so do families of sentences like those on the closed circle of numbered cards mentioned earlier. So far, so good.

But it is clear that this approach, like the others, conflicts drastically with our intuitions concerning the use of the word "true." The use we are trying to explicate is that which is in accord with what is sometimes called the "classical" or "semantic" conception of truth. This is the conception expressed by Aristotle in a well-known passage of the *Metaphysics*:

> To say of what is that it is not, or of what is not that it is, is false, while to say of what is that it is, and of what is not that it is not, is true.[20]

Thus, if I say "It is snowing," what I say is true if and only if it is snowing; and it is false (where "false," as applied to sentences, is just an abbreviation of "not true") if and only if it is not snowing. If I say "It is not snowing," then what I say is true if and only if it is not snowing, and it is false if and only if it is snowing. All of this seems terribly trivial, and it is surprising how often philosophers have challenged it. It sometimes goes by the name of the Correspondence Theory of Truth.

Clearly, we have *one* conception of truth here and not an infinite number of distinct conceptions that could more properly be expressed by an infinite number of truth-predicates. Just as "It is snowing" is true if and only if it is snowing, we expect to say that "Everything in the Bible is true" is true if and only if everything in the Bible is true, regardless of occurrences of the word "true" in the Bible. In other words, statements are true if and only if things are as stated, and this applies even when the subject matter involves truth or falsity. Thus, in using the predicate "true" we do not ordinarily make any tacit or implicit reference to the levels described above. In asserting

Everything in the Bible is true,

the believer very probably has no knowledge of, and no particular concern with, the ways in which the word "true" itself may occur in the Bible; he means simply that, if the Bible says that something is the case, then that's the way it is.

Further evidence that in our ordinary use of "true" and "false" we do not tacitly assume some system of levels has been pointed out by Saul Kripke.[21] Suppose that N says

(1) Nothing that D says about Watergate is true,

and D says

(2) Nothing that N says about Watergate is true.

Each wishes to ascribe falsehood to *all* of the other's asser-
tions, not excepting the statements just mentioned. Now
these two statements can hardly be ruled out as somehow
meaningless, for, as Kripke notes, we can under certain
circumstances determine their truth-values. If, for example, D has made at least one true statement about Watergate [other than (2)], then (1) is clearly false, and (2) will be
true if and only if everything else that N says about Watergate is also false. Other empirical assumptions lead to
other combinations of truth-values for (1) and (2), with the
only excluded combination being that both are true.
Hence (1) and (2) seem meaningful enough, but there is no
way of accommodating them in the described system of
levels.

So much for attempts to obviate the Liar by finding
syntactical restrictions that are plausible and yet suffice to
bar semantic closure of the language. It is no surprise that
such attempts run counter to our intuitions, for, after all,
there seems to be no reason whatever, other than the
threat of the antinomies, why our language should not
include names of its own sentences, together with an unambiguous truth-predicate that is applicable to any and all
sentences and satisfies the Tarskian condition that, by the
very meaning of "true," every equivalence of the form

> X is true if and only if p,

where "p" is replaced by a sentence of the language and
"X" by a structural-descriptive name of the sentence, shall
hold.

TAMPERING WITH LOGIC

We come next to purported solutions of the second type,
involving the alteration of ordinary "two-valued" or "classical" logic.

It should be said at the outset that here again we need
not be surprised if every attempt to find a way out leads to

a violent conflict with intuition. For although, at first thought, the abandonment of the usual laws of logic may not seem too drastic a measure to take in these circumstances, a little reflection and working-out of consequences will convince anyone that this is a domain in which the smallest change may lead to the most unexpected and unwelcome results.

Proposed solutions of the second type try to make capital out of the fact that in the ordinary use of language we sometimes find it inappropriate to apply either the predicate "true" or the predicate "false" to a given sentence even when we know all of the relevant information. Prominent among the various paradigms that have been used to illustrate this phenomenon is the sentence

The present king of France is bald.

This sentence, it is suggested, would be true if the person referred to by the subject term had the property of baldness, and it would be false if that person lacked the property of baldness. But there is no such person; hence, the sentence is neither true nor false. Thus there are sentences, so it is alleged, that fall outside the true-false dichotomy, and the various versions of the Liar sentence are among these. For example,

This sentence is false,

which is syntactically permissible, now loses its sting. We can accept the conclusion that it is true if and only if it is false, because it is neither.

Unfortunately, there is very little agreement on the conditions under which a grammatically acceptable sentence is to be considered neither true nor false. Sentences like the King of France example are supposed to lack truth-value because they *presuppose* something that is not the case—in this instance, that there is such a person as the present king of France. In general, a sentence S is said to presuppose a sentence T if the truth of T is a necessary condition for the truth-or-falsity of S; accordingly, if a presupposition of a sentence S is not true, then S is neither true nor false.[22] However, the only reasonably plausible and nontrivial examples given us are essentially similar to the one mentioned above, where the truth-value gap is said to result from the nonexistence of a referent for the subject term. But clearly this does not apply to A, the Liar sentence; for, once its grammaticality is accepted, it can hardly be said to lack a truth-value because its subject term fails to denote, since its subject term denotes just A itself.

Another class of sentences that are sometimes said to lack truth-value are those involving so-called category mistakes.[23] A typical example would be

The number 3 is red.

Whatever one may feel about this kind of case, it too has no bearing on the Liar sentence, for *sentences* are precisely the category to which the predicate "true" would seem in the first instance to apply. (Or, if propositions or statements are preferred, reformulate A by letting "A" now abbreviate "the proposition expressed by the sentence appearing on line . . . ," etc., or make the analogous change for statements.)

Since A involves neither a so-called category mistake nor a so-called failure of reference, we are still without an intuitive reason for pronouncing A devoid of truth-value. Note that the reason cannot very well be simply that by doing so we escape the antinomy. We require rather to be shown how the Liar sentence essentially resembles some less controversial cases that independently would be plausibly classified as neither true nor false. So far as I am aware, no considerations to that effect have thus far been offered by anyone.

However, even if sense can be made of the proposal to classify certain sentences as neither true nor false, and of the further proposal to include the Liar sentence among these, difficulties will arise when we come to blocking the antinomy. As was observed earlier, in the case of

This sentence is false

the way out via truth-value gaps is obvious, for we can accept the conclusion that it is true if and only if it is false, since it is supposed to be neither. On the other hand, for the formulation

This sentence is not true

and for our old friend A, matters are much less clear. One possibility is to interpret "not" in such a way that the predicate "is not true" becomes just a synonym for "is false." Then the seeming contradiction

A is true if and only if A is not true

will again be acceptable, because neither side will be true. But this is dangerous ground, where it is easy to fall into that bottomless pit of nonsense about which old Socrates used to warn.

For when we were told at the outset that some sentences are neither true nor false, we supposed this to mean that such sentences are not true and are not false. But now it turns out that we are *not* to say that they are not true—for "not true" just means "false," and we are not to say "not false," for that just means "true." So now we have the peculiar result that, although A is neither true nor false,

A is not true

is not true either. Some form of this unwelcome consequence appears, sooner or later, in every truth-value-gap approach to the Liar.

For example, it appears even in Kripke's otherwise excellent paper on truth, which has rightly become a sort of instant classic.[24] Utilizing the idea of truth-value gaps, Kripke constructs an interpreted formalized language L that is consistent and, in a certain sense, contains its own truth-predicate. (In the interpretation, the associated universe of discourse includes the positive integers, and for simplicity we may suppose that for each of these the vocabulary of L contains a numeral that denotes it.) The sentences of L, as interpreted, fall into three disjoint nonempty classes, according as their truth-values are *true, false,* or *undefined.* The claim that L contains its own truth-predicate is explained as meaning that L contains a singulary predicate $T(x)$ which is such that, for every sentence S of L, if p is a numeral that names the Gödel number of S, then

> $T(p)$ is true in L if and only if S is true in L;
> $T(p)$ is false in L if and only if S is false in L;
> and hence
> $T(p)$ is undefined in L if and only if S is
> undefined in L.[25]

Kripke's suggestion is that, as far as the predicate "true" is concerned, this language L reflects our intuitions more faithfully than do the formalized languages previously proposed by Tarski and others. And in several respects—most notably that of containing a purported truth-predicate that is applicable to all sentences of the language, including such sentences as contain that predicate itself—it certainly does.

Before seeing how the aforementioned unwelcome consequence arises in connection with L, however, we need to take note of a bothersome ambiguity involving the word "undefined." The natural use of this word would seem to be such that

> (1) The truth-value of S is undefined

is compatible with, e.g.,

> S is true or false, but its value is unknown

or

> S is true or false, but its value is immaterial.

But in the present use, as regards the language L, it *follows* from (1) that

S is not true and S is not false.

Kripke strenuously resists taking "undefined" as the name of a third truth-value; there seems to me to be no point in arguing about this as long as it is agreed that the three classes of sentences of L are disjoint and exhaustive.[26]

At first glance it looks easy to form various Liar sentences in L. In particular, the vocabulary of L will contain a numeral p which is such that it names the Gödel number of $- T(p)$. According to the semantics of L, the truth-value of this sentence $- T(p)$ is undefined. It follows, as we have noted above, that this sentence is not true in L. Now, since $T(x)$ is being called a "truth-predicate" for L and p is in effect a name of the sentence $- T(p)$, one might suppose that this very fact, viz., that $- T(p)$ is not true in L, is expressed by the sentence $- T(p)$ itself. But it is not so expressed (else the truth-value of $- T(p)$ would be truth, not undefined). So $- T(p)$ does not "say of itself" that it is not true, and, in general, if q is a numeral denoting the number of a sentence of L, $- T(q)$ does not say that that sentence is not true; rather, it says that it is false. It thus appears that, even though certain sentences of L are not true in L, and L contains names of these sentences and also contains a "truth-predicate" $T(x)$ that is applicable to all sentences of L, we cannot use the names and the so-called truth-predicate to state that the nontrue sentences are not true. In my opinion this disqualifies the formal predicate $T(x)$ as a plausible representative of the natural-language predicate "true."[27]

So much for truth-value-gap analyses that also tamper with "not." Clearly, a better idea is to understand "not" in such a way that "is not true" means simply "fails to be true," whether the failure results from falsehood or from lack of truth-value. This is surely the more natural way to use the word "not"; it is the way that has seemed right to most logicians over the past two millennia; and in the context of a truth-value-gap logic it might allow us to block the antinomy while still agreeing that *(iii)* is as contradictory as it looks.

But this natural use of "not" leaves the truth-value-gap approach with no way of challenging the Liar except at step *(i)*. That is, we would have to give up a principle that most philosophers have accepted as a fundamental characterization of the notion of truth, namely, that, by the very meaning of "true," every instance of

X is true if and only if p,

with "p" replaced by a sentence of the language and "X" by a structural-descriptive name of that sentence, shall hold. In particular, we are going to have to say that, since A, which is the right side of the biconditional *(i)*, is neither true nor false, the biconditional *(i)* itself is not true, no matter what status (true, false, or neither) is assigned to its left member. But is this plausible? Hardly. By thinking of "neither true nor false" as "value unknown" or "value immaterial," we can perhaps make sense of the proposal to regard sentences of the form

S if and only if T

as being neither true nor false if either S or T is neither true nor false, provided that S and T are not linked in meaning. But if this last condition is not met, the proposal loses all plausibility. For example, it would be absurd to say that, just because we don't know what the truth-value of a sentence S is, we don't know the truth-value of the sentence

S if and only if S,

for, whether S turns out to be true or to be false, that biconditional will be true. In the same way, there is no plausibility in holding that, because the value of *A* is unknown, the value of *(i)* is unknown; there seems to be no way of dodging the fact that whatever the value of *A* may be discovered to be, the value of *(i)* will have to be *true*.

Tangles like these have led at least one philosopher to attack the Liar at yet another point, namely, the transition from *(i)* and *(ii)* to *(iii)*. [28] This step of the argument rests on Leibniz's Law, which states that terms designating the same thing are interchangeable in any sentence *salva veritate*. Now even Leibniz recognized that this principle will not justify straightforward substitution of identicals in all contexts; clearly, those contexts described by Frege as "indirect" and by Quine as "referentially opaque" must be treated differently. Thus, to cite the classical example: from

> George IV wonders whether Scott is the author of *Waverley*

and

> Scott = the author of *Waverley*

we cannot validly infer

> George IV wonders whether Scott is Scott.

As concerns the Liar, it is proposed that when the logic permits truth-value gaps, Leibniz's Law fails for the context " . . . is true" in the sense that substitution on the basis of a true identity-sentence can take us from a true sentence to one that lacks a truth-value. Applied to our formulation (3), this will allow us to hold that *(i)* and *(ii)* are true regardless of the way we interpret "not," while *(iii)* lacks a truth-value.

But, once again, the price exacted by a proposed solution seems much too high. Apart from troubles associated with the antinomy, there does not appear to be the slightest reason to classify the context " . . . is true" along with all the psychological and modal contexts ordinarily recognized as referentially opaque. From

> S is true

and

> $S = T$

it is paradoxical to refuse to infer

> T is true,

and surely the same should hold when the substitution is made in a molecular sentence like (i).

Before completing our discussion of attempted solutions of the second type, we must acknowledge that in one important respect we may have failed to take seriously enough the claims of those who argue that the natural language is trivalent. They wish to assert, if I understand them correctly, that, in particular, the trivalence applies to the very discourse in which they put forward their views about trivalence. So we must bear in mind that, when people talk this way, we cannot even count on the truth of

> Either every sentence is true or false, or not
> every sentence is true or false.

In fact, there is something odd about their asserting that the Liar sentence is neither true nor false, i.e.,

> A is not true and A is not false,

for this very assertion, according to their doctrine, is itself neither true nor false.

RETREATING INTO THE ABSTRACT

According to William Kneale, "the paradox of the Liar holds no terrors for those who realize how the notion of truth is related to that of a proposition."[29] Many other authors have expressed similar points of view. On grounds having nothing in particular to do with the Liar, they argue, as we have noted earlier, that truth and false-hood do not "properly" apply to sentences but rather to propositions (which are the meanings or senses of sentences) or to statements (which are "made" when meaningful sentences are uttered in certain favorable circumstances). They thus get rid of the Liar by declaring that, although the sentences

> The proposition expressed by this sentence is not true

and

> The statement made by uttering this sentence is not true

are grammatically acceptable, the first expresses no proposition, and/or no statement is made when the second is uttered "in the philosophical way."

There is little agreement about what the ontological status of propositions and statements might be, or even about whether that issue itself makes sense. Sentences, on the other hand, seem universally regarded as classes of similar tokens, which tokens may be sounds or inscriptions; the syntactical properties of sentences (such as those expressed by "contains exactly three words," "is of subject-predicate form," and the like) are relatively easily read off from the perceptible spatiotemporal features of the tokens. For this reason, most logicians end up by dealing with sentences, regardless of their views as to the "proper" subject matter of logic.

Propositions are usually described as the meanings of sentences or as the thoughts that are expressed by sentences. Thus, the same proposition, as we have seen, may be expressed by a number of different sentences in the same or different languages, and to say that a sentence is ambiguous is to say that it may express more than one proposition. Some authors regard propositions as

37

abstract, intensional entities, which, like sets and numbers, are supposed to have an objective existence in Plato's heaven independent of ourselves and even independent of whether or not there are any sentences to express them. When such authors identify propositions with thoughts, they are considering thoughts not as particular psychological states of individual human beings but rather as the common property of people who succeed in communicating with one another by means of sentences.[30] Another group of authors, to which Russell belongs, do regard propositions as certain psychological states of individuals and hence as mind-dependent.[31] Still others regard all such issues as entirely specious; they argue that the word "proposition" has a perfectly intelligible use *in particular contexts* (e.g., as in "'It is raining' and 'Es regnet' express the same proposition" and "Jones has an attitude of belief toward the proposition that all men are mortal"), but that it is not the kind of word that has meaning in isolation or that "stands for an entity."

However that may be, the dominant view nowadays is that statements, and neither sentences nor propositions, are properly the bearers of truth and falsehood. We are told that the same sentence, with the same meaning, may be used on different occasions to make different statements. The sentence "He did it" would be an example of this. It can also happen that different sentences, with clearly different meanings, are used on the same or different occasions to make the same statement. For example, if you say, "Nobody knows the trouble I've seen," and I say, with reference to you, "Nobody knows the trouble he's seen," we are deemed to have made the same statement by uttering sentences that do not have the same meaning. So statements are not to be confused with sentences or with propositions. When they are hypostatized, however, they turn out to be much more like propositions than like sentences: although they are said to have many of the features that more obviously apply to sentences—e.g., to be of subject-predicate form, to contain descriptions, to be positive or negative, singular, general, and so on—these features of the statements cannot be read off in any simple way from the features of the sentences used in making them. Thus, any statement that can be made by uttering a singular sentence (e.g., "Socrates is wise") can also be made by uttering a logically equivalent general sentence (e.g., "Anybody who is not wise is not Socrates"), and similar difficulties prevent a simple reading-off in the other cases, too.

Fortunately, for our present purposes it is not necessary to discuss critically the considerations favoring one or another of the various candidates for the position of primary truth-bearer.[32] For, so far as I can see, in relation to the Liar there are only two relevant possibilities: *either* propositions (or statements, as the case may be) are essentially abstract doubles of grammatically correct sentences, so that we can perfectly well have a proposition (or statement) that directly or indirectly asserts its own nontruth, *or* for some reason there cannot be such a proposition (or statement).

In the first case, the Liar reappears with all its force, and the shift from sentences to the more abstract entities will not materially affect the plausibility or implausibility of the various proposed solutions we have discussed.

In the second case, we require a good reason *why* there are no propositions or statements of the types that lead to the Liar. That reason, if I may belabor the point, cannot be simply the ad hoc pronouncement that to allow such propositions or statements is to open the door to the antinomy. Something more is required. But, since nobody pretends that propositions and statements ever (unless possibly, in a few extremely rudimentary cases, like "I am hungry") appear to us directly, i.e., without their sentential clothing, we shall need some way of knowing *in advance* whether using a given sentence is going to get us into trouble because there will be no corresponding proposition or statement. That is, we need some practicable criterion for determining which sentences, on which occasions, will have corresponding propositions or statements. I say *Practicable* criterion, for it will not do to tell us "Go ahead and use the sentence; if you get into trouble, that shows that there was no proposition or that you didn't manage to make a statement, which is why you got into trouble." That would be like:

> "Why won't my watch run?"
> "Because it is defective."
> "How can I recognize a defective watch so that I won't have this problem again?"
> "Observe whether it continues to run; if it does, well and good; if it doesn't, that shows it's defective, which is why it won't run."

In sum, it appears that nothing is really gained by the retreat to propositions and statements. For either our sentences are, as it were, perfect pictures of their abstract counterparts, in which case the problem of finding a way to recognize the bad actors in the one domain amounts to that of finding a way to recognize their fellows in the other; or, the culprit sentences give rise to the antinomy because they have no abstract counterparts, in which case our problem may simply be redescribed as that of finding a way of determining which sentences have no such counterparts.

SOME RELATED PARADOXES

The Liar has many relatives, some closer than others. The Barber paradox,[33] for example, although it superficially resembles the Liar, hardly deserves the name "paradox," for it is merely a proof that there is no such barber; nobody will be surprised that this is the case or even that it is provably the case. The antinomy described on page 24, above, on the other hand, is so close a relative that it is perhaps best thought of as just another form of the same argument. Between these extremes we find arguments like the Epimenides, which, though they are not antinomies, appear to prove something that should not be provable by logic alone.

For another example, let the letter "S" stand for —i.e., name—the sentence

S is not a necessary truth.

Then it would seem that S both is and is not a necessary truth. It is not, for, if it were, it would be true and hence would not be a necessary truth; but we have just proved S a priori, and so it is a necessary truth after all. [34] Or, let "S" stand for

Nobody knows that S is true.

Suppose that S is not true. Then somebody knows that S is true, and hence S is true. Thus we have proved that S is true, although, oddly enough, we have also shown that nobody knows that this is the case. Or, let "S" stand for

Either the reader has no slightest doubt that
S is true, or S is not true.

Suppose, again, that S is not true. Since S is a disjunction, this implies that neither of its disjuncts is true, and hence S is true. Therefore, S is indeed true. But then its right disjunct is false. Consequently, the left disjunct must be true, and we have now proved that, whatever the reader may think, he has no slightest doubt that S is true. Clearly, by substituting any arbitrarily chosen sentence T for the left disjunct, we can construct an analogous a priori proof of T.

In each of these cases we feel, perhaps, that there is something quite wrong with letting the sentence refer directly or indirectly to its own truth. But compare the following. Let "S" stand for

S does not follow from P,

where "P" names some set of true sentences, to be thought of as a set of axioms. Now suppose that S follows from P. Then since the sentences P are true, S is also true and hence does not follow from P after all. If P is the set of all true sentences, we have in effect the Liar; because for S to say of itself that it does not follow from P will be equivalent to saying of itself that it is not true. But, if P is, e.g., a set of axioms for arithmetic, and if we find a way to express S as a sentence of arithmetic, we have the core of Gödel's profound argument showing that no consistent set of axioms for arithmetic suffices to yield all and only the truths of arithmetic as theorems.

Thus, the boundary line between the profound and the merely paradoxical is alarmingly difficult to find.

RUSSELL'S ANTINOMY

Russell's Antinomy has a much shorter history than the antinomy of the Liar, dating only from 1905. But it is at least equally puzzling, and it has had an enormous influence on subsequent work in logic and the foundations of mathematics.

To present this antinomy in an efficacious way, we must first say a few words about the intuitive concepts of *class* (or *set*) and *member* (or *element*). Anyone who attempts to define these concepts soon discovers that the task is surprisingly difficult; it seems that we are forced either to employ terms that are practically synonymous with (and even less clear than) the terms to be defined, or to introduce misleading implications that must be disavowed in codicils to the definition, or both. Consider, for example, the following definition, offered by Georg Cantor, the father of what is now called "set theory": "a set [*Menge*] is a collection into a whole [*Zusammenfassung zu einem Ganzen*] of definite, distinct objects of our intuition or our thought. The objects are called the members [*Elemente*] of a set." As explicated by Abraham Fraenkel,

the term "definite" in this definition means that given a set M it should be at least intrinsically determined for any object whether that object is a member of M or not; "distinct" stresses that any two members of a set are different, as contrasted with a sequence, in which the same member may occur repeatedly.[35]

Further provisos must be added. The term "collection," which is close to being a synonym of "class," unfortunately suggests collecting, or bringing the collected objects into spatial proximity, whereas no such condition on membership in a class is intended. Further, the expression "objects of our intuition or our thought" may seem to limit the membership of classes to objects of which we think or are in some other manner aware, whereas presumably we human beings think of, at most, a very small portion of what there is in the universe, and thus there are many classes containing elements we do not even suspect to exist. It is clear that most of the attempted definitions of *class* are best understood, not as definitions in any proper sense of that term, but merely as attempts to draw our attention to various essential features of this fundamental concept. Let us continue with some of the "definitive" statements that are made in this vein.

Any thing or things whatever constitute the entire membership of a class; in other words, for any things there are, there is exactly one class having just those things as members. To the classes covered by this characterization we must add one more—the empty class, i.e., the unique class having no members at all. Usually classes are referred to by means of *conditions* satisfied by their membership; thus, the class of human beings has as members those and only those things satisfying the condition "x is a human being," and the class of planets in the solar system is the class of those and only those things satisfying the condition "x is a planet in the solar system."But there is no a priori reason why, for every class, there should be (in English or any other language) a condition determining the membership of that class; indeed, one of Cantor's best-known theorems shows that there are more classes than there are conditions in any language whatever. (It would of course be possible to retreat into the abstract again, making of conditions something analogous to propositions. Then, emptily, we could say that, for every class, there is a condition satisfied by just the elements of that class.)

From the metaphysical side, which is almost impossible to ignore when one attempts an intuitive characterization of this concept, a class is an abstract entity, having no spatial position, mass, shape, or temporal location or extent; like numbers and geometrical figures, it is supposed to exist independently of our thoughts and even independently of our own existence. Classes are not in any way themselves accessible to sensory perception, though our thinking about them may be facilitated by the perception of certain sentences or diagrams, just as, in thinking about geometrical entities, we may be helped by looking at chalk marks on blackboards. The essential role of these perceptible items, according to the original Platonic account, is primarily to amuse the body for awhile so that the mind can view the abstract entities without being distracted by the never-ending series of demands the body puts upon it.

We must carefully distinguish the member-class relation from that of part to whole. Indeed, I suspect that confusion about this matter is what gives many people the confidence that they are well acquainted with classes. The part-whole relation is transitive; if your thumb is part of your hand and your hand is part of your body, it follows that your thumb is part of your body. This sort of transitivity does not in general characterize the relation of member to class. The number two is a member of the class of even numbers, and the class of even numbers is a member of the class of all infinite classes of numbers; but the number two is not a member of the latter class, for two is not an infinite class of numbers. Thus "member of" and "part of" denote two quite different relations.

Correspondingly, one must in general distinguish between a given class, on the one hand, and the whole or heap made up of the members of that class. Consider, for example, one of those pyramidal stacks of Civil War cannonballs that are to be seen on the lawns in front of old courthouses in the Midwest. Such a stack will contain, say, thirty cannonballs; like each of the cannonballs, it is a physical object; it has a mass that is approximately thirty times that of an individual ball, and it has a location in space, a shape, a center of gravity, etc. The class of those thirty objects, on the other hand, is an abstract entity, lacking all the characteristics just mentioned. It has no more claim to be identified with the heap than do many other classes—e.g., the class of all molecules that are parts of those cannonballs, or the class of all atoms that are contained in those molecules. These various classes, having different numbers of members, are clearly distinct from one another. Therefore, they cannot *all* be identified with the heap, and a little reflection shows that *none* should be so identified.

Introductions to set theory sometimes contribute to such confusions by citing, as paradigm examples of sets or classes, such things as a bunch of grapes, a herd of sheep, or a box of apples.[36] They would perhaps do better, for purposes of getting across the essential idea, to make up a class from one of the grapes, one of the sheep, a seed from the grape, an apple, and the moon. At any rate, it seems important to disabuse students, early on, of any notion that they have ever *seen* a class, whether in a vineyard or out in the fields, unless the "seeing" was done with the "mind's eye," as is sometimes recommended.

One last point, before we come to the antinomy, concerns matters of *existence*. Strictly speaking, there is only one class of which we can properly say that its members do not exist, and that is the empty (or null) class. Thus "the class whose members are the present king and queen of France" and "the class whose members are Santa Claus and the Easter Rabbit" are just a pair of descriptions of the null class. So also are "the class of characters in *Hamlet*," "the class of Greek gods," and maybe even "the class of positive integers."

Now, this last example verges on the heretical; and before we are excommunicated by the mathematicians, we had better offer some explanation of how, if in reality the class of positive integers is empty, we can customarily and correctly say that it has infinitely many members. The answer, I believe, is to be found in a general feature of our use of language in plays, novels, and other fictional representations. The actors in a play speak *as though* the characters and other fictional objects existed, and we, the audience, enter temporarily into the spirit of the thing, as it were. In reading a novel or other work of fiction, we for a time join the author in playing his game. If someone says, "Zeus was really on the side of the Trojans," we don't reply, "That's surely false, because Zeus never existed," for that would be queer in the same way that it would be queer for the quarterback to try to hit the ball out of the park for a home run. When we are playing the *Iliad-Odyssey* Greek-myth game, we talk as though all the *dramatis personae* of those stories were real; in that context, if we employ the language of classes, we shall be saying that the class having Zeus, Hector, and Greater Ajax as members is a class with three elements, even though we know perfectly well that it is in fact empty. In the same way, even if we are skeptical about the existence of abstract entities, including classes and numbers, we shall not, during the play, loudly declare that the class of prime numbers is a nonexistent combination of nonexistent things; such an expostulation—like "They're only actors!" —would merely earn us angry looks from the rest of the audience.

So, back to the story about classes. We have said that, for any things there are, there is exactly one class having just those things as members. Thus, classes themselves are to be members of classes. In fact, a class may turn out to be a member of itself, though it seems that most are not. The class of all classes containing more than a thousand members is clearly a member of itself; the same holds for the class of all abstract entities, the class of all things not in my pocket, and the class described as follows:

> The class of all things mentioned on lines 16 and 17 of page 47 of *Skeptical Essays*.

On the other hand, the class of men is not a man, the class of dogs is not a dog, and the class of prime numbers is not a prime number. These latter are therefore examples of classes that are not members of themselves.

Consider, now, the class whose members are those and only those classes that are not members of themselves. Call this class "R"; whether R is large, small, or even empty is immaterial to the argument. If R is a member of itself, then it is not a member of itself (for its members are precisely those classes that are not members of themselves), and, if it is not, then it is (for the same reason); therefore, R is a member of itself if and only if R is not a member of itself, which is a contradiction.

That is Russell's Antinomy in its simplest form. Like the Liar, it appears also in many other versions, so that no solution may be based on the peculiarities of this one. In its simplest form, the condition that gives rise to the unruly class R is

> x is not a member of x;

R is the class of all things satisfying that condition. But an infinite number of other conditions will give rise to the antinomy in a similar way, e.g., the conditions

> x is a member of no class that is a member of x

and

> x is a member of some class all of whose members are not members of x,

among others.

It should be noted that the antinomy involves, at most, what is nowadays called "abstract set theory," i.e., that part of the general theory of classes that can be formulated without using any nonlogical predicate other than "is a member of." Thus, even if we abandon all assumptions as to the existence of nonclasses—points, numbers, atoms, people, or whatever—so that only classes will be members of classes, the antinomy will still appear.

What is more, one might even say that the problem has nothing particularly or essentially to do with classes and the relation "is a member of." For, consider any domain D and any binary relation E among the individuals of D: there cannot be an individual in D that bears the relation E to those and only those individuals in D that do not bear the relation E to themselves. (For, if there were one, it would bear E to itself if and only if it did not bear E to itself.) By choosing different domains and different relations, we get a large number of particular cases, some of which are puzzling while others are not. Thus, there cannot be a barber who shaves those and only those men who do not shave themselves; no bibliography of bibliographies can list those and only those bibliographies that do not list themselves; no country can finance all those and only those countries that do not finance themselves; and so on. The only surprising aspect of these cases is that we can prove the nonexistence without using any empirical information.

The antinomies, on the other hand, arise in the cases in which we also have a priori grounds for asserting the existence of the individuals in question. This is the situation with respect to the class of all classes that are not members of themselves. For, since any thing or things constitute a class, why should not the thing or things (even if there are none) that satisfy any given condition constitute a class? Similarly, the property of being a property that does not apply to itself will generate an antinomy, for why should there not be such a property?

As one more example to illustrate the point of the preceding paragraphs, let us call sentences of the form "No S is P" negative generalizations, and let us say that such a generalization *holds of* an individual I if and only if I is not an exception to the rule expressed by the generalization. Thus, "No ravens are white" holds of an individual raven if and only if that raven is not white. Now taking these generalizations as our domain D, and taking *"holds of"* as denoting our binary relation E, we can prove that no generalization holds of those and only those generalizations that do not hold of themselves. But what about the following generalization?

No generalization holds of itself.

If this holds of itself, it is not an exception and hence does not hold of itself. If it does not hold of itself, it *is* an exception to the rule it states and hence does hold of itself. With this, we are nearly back to the Liar.

SOLUTIONS

It is neither appropriate nor feasible here to give more than a sketchy account of the main directions in which ways of coping with Russell's Antinomy have been sought.[37] Most of the work has been done by mathematicians attempting to salvage enough of the general theory of classes—sometimes called "naïve set theory" or "Cantor's paradise"— to serve as a foundation for all or most of classical mathematics. Their efforts, which have led to the study and solution of some very deep problems, have certainly not been crowned with success, if "to succeed" means in this case to clarify and sharpen the concept of class to such an extent that the mistake giving rise to the antinomy becomes evident for all to see. (This is the sense of "succeed" in which, for example, Cantor succeeded in clarifying the notion of "equinumerous" so as to make it obvious that a class can be equinumerous with a proper subclass of itself.) On the other hand, very ingenious theories have been constructed that do in fact block the antinomy and are sufficiently rich to provide a foundation for mathematics, though they all have in common the feature that, besides excluding the antinomy, they also exclude much other substance that is apparently harmless.

For the most part, attempts to deal with the antinomy have utilized one of three methods. Either (1) by some form of the so-called Theory of Types they disallow as meaningless the expression "x is not a member of x" and the other related expressions that give rise to the contradiction, i.e., they rule out these expressions on grammatical grounds; or (2) they accept the suspect expressions as meaningful, but, giving up the principle that for every condition there is a corresponding class, they arrange that there shall be no corresponding classes in these cases; or (3) they accept the conditions and the corresponding classes, but, giving up another intuitively obvious principle, they pronounce these classes incapable of membership in any class.

The Theory of Types, of which there are many different versions, was the remedy favored by Russell himself. It is best understood as a theory about language, though there is no doubt that it was originally intuitively appealing as an ontological doctrine. For it asserts (in its simplest version) that the contents of the world are, first of all, individuals, then classes of those individuals, then classes of those classes, and so on. The individuals are of type 0, the classes of individuals are of type 1, and, in general, classes of classes of type n are of type $n + 1$. The individuals are considered so fundamentally different from the classes of individuals, and the latter from the classes of classes of individuals, and so on, that to assert or deny the membership relation between any but entities of adjacent ascending types is deemed not merely false but nonsensical.

Now, it will be noticed that this account itself easily runs into paradox, for it bases linguistic rules on an ontological doctrine that the rules then forbid us from stating. For example, if we ask why the sentence "The class of dogs is a member of the class of dogs" is nonsensical and not merely false, we are told that the class of dogs differs *toto caelo* from any dog, i.e., is not a dog, i.e., is not a member of itself.[38] Because of these and other difficulties, the Theory of Types is better presented as a doctrine that apportions the linguistic expressions (instead of the individuals and classes) into types. The expressions we intend to use as names or variables for individuals are assigned type 0 and, in general, if, from the ontological point of view, type n was assigned to certain entities, it is now assigned to the expressions that are to be thought of as standing for or ranging over those entities. An expression of the form "x is a member of y" is accepted as grammatical if and only if the expression x is of one type lower than the expression y.[39]

Clearly, this device does exclude as ungrammatical the expression "x is not a member of x" and the other conditions that give rise to Russell's Antinomy, and in comparison with the aforementioned methods (2) and (3) it has certain important advantages. First and foremost, it has intuitive appeal independently of its effectiveness in blocking the antinomy. Many people feel that to say such things as "7 is blue" or "The class of dogs has a lame leg" is not simply to utter falsehoods—like "7 is an even number" and "The class of dogs has exactly 333 members"—but to talk nonsense. This sort of nonsense even has a special name, as we have seen: "category mistake."[40] So the limitations by means of which the first method avoids the antinomy lack the ad hoc quality that is so prominent in the other approaches. Also, this method offers the advantages of unrestricted class abstraction: for any condition there will be a corresponding class, so that all difficulties in proving the existence or elementhood of classes are removed.

On the other hand, even in its simplest form the Theory of Types introduces many unwelcome complications. There will be infinitely many universal sets and infinitely many empty sets corresponding, respectively, to the infinitely many expressions "$x = x$" and "$x \neq x$," one pair for each type. The relations of identity and difference will be similarly multiplied, and yet, even with this plethora of identity and difference relations, we shall be unable to express such a proposition as that the class of dogs is not a dog. If the positive integers are defined in the usual way as classes of classes, there will be a distinct complete set of these integers at every type from 2 on up, but again, even with all this duplication, we shall be unable to say, e.g., that the class whose members are 7 and 5 is equinumerous with the class whose members are the sun and the moon. Other forms of Type Theory have been invented that avoid some of these disadvantages, but invariably they introduce their own collections of intuitive defects and technical inconveniences.

The leading example of method (2) is the Zermelo-Fraenkel set theory. In this approach the full notation of the theory of classes (i.e., all expressions that can be built up by truth-functional composition and quantification from atomic components of the form "x is a member of y") is accepted as meaningful, but there is in general no guarantee that, corresponding to a given condition, there will be a class of all things satisfying that condition. In place of such a guarantee there is now incorporated a principle assuring only the existence of a class of all things that satisfy the condition *and* are members of some class. By itself this principle establishes only the existence of the empty class (take "$x \neq x$" as the condition), so grist for the mill has to be provided by other axioms in which the existence of various kinds of classes is stipulated, sometimes unconditionally, sometimes contingently upon the existence of other classes. In this way we obtain classes corresponding to a large number of conditions. One of the axioms specifies that all classes are "grounded," i.e., that there is no class that has a member that has a member that has a member . . . and so on ad infinitum. This blocks the existence of classes corresponding to "x is a member of x," "x is a member of some y that is a member of x," and various other suspect conditions. The nonexistence of classes corresponding to the conditions that lead to the antinomy is of course provable by the argument of the antinomy itself. Thus there is no class of just those classes satisfying "x is not a member of x," for, if there were such a class, it would have to be a member of itself if and only if it was not a member of itself.

Thus the axioms of Zermelo-Fraenkel set theory assert the existence of classes corresponding to certain conditions and deny that of classes corresponding to others. But for a large number of conditions they do not settle the matter one way or the other. Hence it is clear that, while all of the axioms do seem intuitively true, they constitute only a small part (albeit an important part) of the truth about classes. The only classes whose existence they guarantee are grounded on a single "individual," the empty class. This suffices for the foundation of classical mathematics, but that does not mean that the axioms constitute an "implicit" characterization of the notions of class and membership. To say that they do would be no more satisfactory than to attempt to define "human being" by saying that Socrates is a human being and that all descendants of human beings are human beings. Too much is left out. Not only does this approach give no independently intuitive reason for denying the existence of classes corresponding to the antinomy-producing conditions (while accepting the existence of various classes corresponding to conditions in which some of the culprit conditions are components), but, without any intuitive justification whatever, it fails to provide classes for multitudes of conditions that seem perfectly innocuous. Thus, considered as an explication of the concepts of class and member, it seems even more deficient than approaches utilizing some form of the Theory of Types, for the latter at least allow unlimited class abstraction once the range of meaningful expressions has been specified.

Method (3), of which the set theory of von Neumann and Bernays is the most prominent example, shares most of the disadvantages of method (2). However, there is now a class for every condition, so the defect of having no classes for most grammatically acceptable conditions is remedied. However, a new puzzler is introduced: most classes are to be generically incapable of membership in *any* class, let alone in themselves. Again, it seems that no intuitively satisfactory reason can be given why some classes should have this extraordinary property; for that any thing or things constitute the membership of a class is, as we have said, fundamental to the very notions of class and member. Of course, the *motivation* for making such exemptions is to block the antinomy, but motivation is not justification. No one will be satisfied with the explanation that (a) the defect in the argument leading to Russell's Antinomy is that the class R is erroneously assumed to be capable of membership, and (b) the reason why the class R is not capable of membership is that Russell's Antinomy would result if it were.

It is not surprising, therefore, that none of these

methods—nor any of their multifarious variations—has won anything like the majority approval by the mathematicians and philosophers who have studied the problem. Still less approval has been achieved by methods that tamper with the underlying logic, e.g., by introducing truth-value gaps or by modifying the operation of negation. Undeniably, the standard set theories are monuments to the ingenuity of the human mind in rescuing important portions of the general or "naïve" theory of classes, but, as noted earlier, they do not leave us with any feeling of insight that our concepts of class and member have been refined or sharpened in such a way as to show where the error lay that generated the contradiction. All that we can say is that these basic concepts have turned out to be incoherent and that there seem to be no similar concepts of equal power and generality that can be put in their place.[41]

The Moral

It is time now to draw some conclusions from the two examples we have been considering.

As stated at the outset, my purpose in discussing these antinomies is to convince or remind the reader of a very important fact about rational discourse, namely, that it is possible to have impeccable arguments for both sides of a contradiction—"impeccable" in the sense that the reasoning is as clear and exact as what is accepted in the most rigorous argumentation elsewhere and that the premises are exclusively the kind of statements we consider to be true by virtue of the very meanings of the terms they contain.

Now it is very natural and reasonable to suppose that, if we are confronted with a pair of arguments leading to opposite conclusions, at least one of the arguments must have at least one of the following flaws: either it contains an instance of an invalid mode of inference, or it contains a false premise, or some crucial ingredient is ambiguous, vague, or ungrammatical. Indeed, this point of view might even be considered essential to rationality.

Leibniz was in effect the first to call attention to the fact that there is another important way, besides those listed above, in which arguments can fail to be logically sound. Namely, if any of the constituent concepts are singly or jointly incoherent, we can have the result that contradictory or otherwise unwelcome conclusions may be derived by sound inference patterns from premises that qualify as necessary truths, i.e., as true by virtue of their meanings alone.

As will be remembered, Leibniz held that in any true proposition of the form "A is B" the predicate concept B is contained, expressly or virtually, in the subject concept A. But he noticed that the converse generalization, that if B is contained in A, then "A is B" is true, holds only if the concept A contains no incompatible components.[42] Thus, although propositions of the form "AB is B" or "$ABCD$ is C" are for the most part necessary truths, this fails in those exceptional cases in which the subject term is inconsistent. For example, "A black dog is a dog" and "A short fat man is fat" are necessary truths, but "A married bachelor is married" is not. The latter amounts to "A married unmarried man is married," which, as regards necessity, is on a par with "A married unmarried man is unmarried." With such cases in mind, Leibniz insisted that, if we hope to prove "A is B" by showing that the concept B is contained in the concept A, we must include a demonstration that the concept A is consistent. As is well known, he applied this requirement in particular to the ontological argument for the existence of God, saying that, to be conclusive, it needs the addition of a demonstration—which he endeavored to supply—that the concept of God is internally consistent.

Therefore, in considering our antinomies, and especially in considering the classical philosophical problems to which the following chapters are devoted, we should take into account the possibility that the best diagnosis of the trouble is that the fundamental concepts involved—e.g., those of truth, class, moral responsibility, and "external world"—are radically defective in the sense that, the clearer we get about them, the clearer it becomes that they lead to contradiction and must be repaired, if possible, or, failing that, replaced.

2

THE FREEDOM
OF THE WILL

Like any other problem, the problem of the Freedom of the Will can be formulated in many ways.[1] In fact, the diversity of statements and associated definitions that philosophers have offered under this heading is so great that in some cases it seems more natural to say that certain ingredient terms are being used in different senses than to describe the given statements as different versions of the same problem.

I shall consider that we have before us two formulations of a single problem rather than two wholly different problems when there is a simple and obvious method that will transform any solution of either into a solution of the other. Of course it is often possible to notice that there is such a method even when one does not have in hand a solution to either version. This applies in particular to the Free Will problem, where, if I am right, nobody has found an acceptable solution to any version.

THE PROBLEM

In one of its simplest forms the problem has been presented as follows. Every event is the effect of antecedent events, and these in turn are caused by events antecedent to them, and so on, as far back in time as one may choose to go. Human actions are no exception to this rule; for, although the causes of some of them are much less well understood than the causes of certain other types of event, it can hardly be denied that they do have causes and that these causes determine their effects with the same certainty and inevitability that are found in every other kind of case. In particular, those human actions usually called *free* are, each of them, the ultimate and inevitable effect of events occurring long before the agent was born and over which he obviously had no control; and, since he could not prevent the existence of the causes, it is clear that he could not avoid the occurrence of the effects. Consequently, despite appearances to the contrary, human actions are no more free than the motion of the tides or the rusting of a piece of iron that is exposed to water and air.[2]

Thus if, for example, it is asked what essential difference there is between my action in "freely" saying "Yes" when you talk me into a game of cards and my action in saying "Ouch!" when you stamp on my toe, the answer is: none. In one case the vocal mechanism is actuated by a relatively simple sequence of neural events leading from a violent stimulation of nerve endings in my toe; in the other, the process is more complicated, involving *inter alia* a stimulation of the auditory nerves that results from the impact upon the eardrums of condensations and rarefactions of the surrounding air. But—not to minimize the difference between being struck by a solid object and being "bombarded" with words—it is clear that the precise way in which the cause produces the effect is not relevant here. Nor is the fact that, in general, we have a much less adequate or detailed understanding of the mechanisms by which our so-called free acts are produced than of those accounting for the rest of what we do. Indeed, it is this very ignorance, and not an essential difference between the kinds of action, that encourages our vain attempts to make the distinction, as witness the fact that, the more knowledge we obtain of the causal chain leading back from a given action to a set of events that were clearly beyond the agent's control, the less confidence we have in holding that he acted "freely."

Therefore, if, as seems hardly to require explicit statement, we are morally responsible for only those of our actions that are done freely, or, to put it even more conservatively, if we are not responsible for actions we cannot help doing, then it follows that nobody is morally responsible for anything.

SOLUTIONS

Even in formulations as relatively unsophisticated as the foregoing, the problem has elicited a wide variety of mutually incompatible responses from the philosophers who have dealt with it. The very notion of *causation* has been attacked as an outmoded, anthropomorphic relic of primitive thought, unfit for modern science, which is said to employ instead the concept *functional relationship*. (Whether the motion of the moon, together with other factors, causes the motion of the tides, or vice versa, is said to be an issue without real content; the important fact is that the two motions vary functionally with each other.) Or, the *notion* of causation is accepted, but it is simply denied that every event is the effect of antecedent causes, exceptions being made for human volitions and certain subsequent actions. Or, it is agreed that events, including human actions, are indeed always the effects of antecedent causes, but it is denied that these causes determine their effects with anything more than statistical probability. Or again, in a desperate attempt to make room for "free" actions, it is argued that, while the physical world is completely deterministic or nearly so, the events that constitute the realm of thought are much less rigidly connected with their mental and physical antecedents.